# Matthew

## ·A·VOYAGE·FROM·THE·PAST·INTO·THE·FUTURE·

## Newfoundland and home again to Bristol.

## A celebration of the voyage of the replica of John Cabot's Caravel.

*Compiled by*
*Steve Martin and Colin Sanger*

It was around 1494 that the Italian navigator Giovanni Caboto went to the court of King Henry VII of England seeking sponsorship for a voyage to the west, to try to open an easier trading route to the silks and spices of Asia.

Having been turned down by the kings of Spain and Portugal, who he approached with his idea, he went instead to England and impressed King Henry VII with his maps and visions of wealth.

On 5th March 1496 Henry granted 'the well-beloved John Cabote' or John Cabot, as his name had become anglicized, Letters Patent' to 'seeke out, discover and finde whatsoever isles, countries, regions or provinces . . . which before this time have been unknown to all Christians'.

Backed by the wealthy merchants of Bristol as well as the king, Cabot set sail in the fifty ton *Matthew* with a crew of nineteen including about fourteen 'hearty Bristol sailors'. He didn't find his intended China or Japan but instead discovered the New Founde Landes'.

After anchoring the *Matthew* off the shore of this New World, Cabot and a small party rowed ashore to erect a cross and the banners of Henry VII, the Pope and St. Mark of Venice at a place they named Bonavista. They didn't venture inland but sailed over nine hundred miles down the coast of North America, before heading east again and discovering the Grand Banks fishery on the way home, a cod fishery so rich that it stimulated the English colonisation of North America.

# FOREWORD

Who would have believed that building a replica wooden ship would have such a profound effect on the City of Bristol and its citizens.

I could write for hours about the ship, the organisers, the organisation, the events but the book tells you all those things. I want to write about the feelings it created in the City amongst its citizens; feelings of pride, joy and unity.

The citizens of Bristol turned out in their thousands for all the major milestones in the ship's construction and sailing life. I well remember that glorious September evening in 1995 when *Matthew* was launched when even the weather was perfect. Thousands of my fellow Bristolians lined the quayside and the bridges to view *Matthew* being gently lowered into the water. You could almost touch the pride that this small wooden ship created in the City. This feeling was enhanced when, during the Festival of the Sea, *Matthew* was towed into the harbour with lights playing on the rigging, the spontaneous cheering from tens of thousands of well-wishers, created such a sense of pride, joy and unity that my whole body tingled and my eyes watered. Judging by the smiles on peoples' faces at the end of the evening I am sure this was the same for everyone.

It is very appropriate that *Matthew* should return to her home port of Bristol, when her historic voyage was completed in September 1998.The City historically has been known internationally by the phrase, 'Ship Shape and Bristol Fashion'. *Matthew* has certainly built on that reputation.

Graham Robertson
Lord Mayor of Bristol

# The Matthew Project

St. John Hartnell

Chairman
Cabot 500 Celebrations
and
The Matthew Project

'Early in 1991 I was approached by Tony Shepherd, the President of the Bristol Initiative, and Councillor Graham Robertson, the Leader of the Bristol City Council to see if I would be Chairman of a Joint Venture company that the City and the Initiative were forming to celebrate the 500th Anniversary of John Cabot's historic voyage to Newfoundland from Bristol and if possible to organise the construction of a replica of Cabot's ship, *Matthew*.

The statue of John Cabot on the dockside in Bristol.

It was a challenge that I could not refuse! During the next twelve months and with a lot of help from many people, I gradually formed the plans for what has been an exciting and very rewarding time.

His Royal Highness The Prince Philip, Duke of Edinburgh, generously agreed to be Patron to the Project which he saw as one commemorating the quincentenary of the start of the Colonies, the start of the Commonwealth, and most importantly the start of the spread of the English spoken language.

The route of the replica Matthew from Bristol to Newfoundland

# m atthew

| | | Air draft (without topm... |
|---|---|---|
| Ship type | Caravel | |
| Crew (including captain) | 19 | Air draft (including to... |
| Masts | 3 plus bowsprit | Displacement (unloade... |
| Length (including castle) | 73 feet | Displacement |
| Length (hull) | 63 feet 11 inches | Sail area |
| Length (waterline) | 61 feet 6 inches | Keel |
| Beam (hull) | 19 feet 8 inches | Frames |
| Beam (over all) | 20 feet 6 inches | Underwater planking |
| Draft | 7 feet | Topsides/decking |

ICELAND

ATLANTIC

OCEAN

IRELAND

ENGLAND

Bristol

# FACTS AND FIGURES

| | | |
|---|---|---|
| et | Masts/spars | Douglas fir |
| et | Registered tonnage | 58·38 tons |
| tons | Cruising speed (power) | 6 knots (flat water) |
| ns | Cruising speed (sail) | 4 knots |
| square feet | | |
| e (African hardwood) | | |
| sh oak | | |
| ish larch | | |
| las fir | | |

*Would you like to learn more about building and sailing the replica Matthew, or more about John Cabot and his links with Bristol?*

*By joining the Matthew Society you will support the Matthew Project and keep up with all that is going on with this exciting venture.*

In 1992 an old friend of mine, Peter Workman, joined the company as Director General and we set up an office and got down to business in earnest. Colin Mudie, the naval architect, researched the design of the *Matthew* and drew plans of the three masted caravel that she is today.

In 1992 we visited Brest's Festival of the Sea and decided that we would hold a similar International Festival of the Sea in Bristol in 1996. The purpose was to support the *Matthew* and to raise public awareness in the project and the ship.

Whilst the City of Bristol were being extremely supportive of my plans, they had no funds that they could make available and any money needed for the Project had to be raised by donation or sponsorship. In the autumn of 1993 another long standing friend stepped in and made the whole project possible. Michael Slade, the managing director of Helical Bar plc, a fine sailor, generously agreed to underwrite through Helical Bar, the entire cost of the *Matthew* Project and the Festival of the Sea. This enabled me to fire the starting pistol which led to our employing the shipwrights, properly appointing Colin Mudie and setting the whole process into motion.

On 20th May 1994 His Royal Highness The Prince Philip, Duke of Edinburgh, came to Bristol and at a fitting ceremony laid the keel of the ship. The City had made available a marvellous and prominent site at Redcliffe Quay upon which we had built a fine canopy under which the ship could be constructed, with a splendid Visitor Centre behind. Bristol finally realised that my plans were not mythical and that *Matthew* would be built and that we would have a Festival of the Sea.

The City lent us a well located building in the docks which we quickly adapted as our offices, Charles Payton joined as the Director in charge of the Festival of the Sea and our plans progressed swiftly. On 9th September 1995 the ship was launched at a magnificent ceremony and Bristol celebrated.

In 1996 the *Matthew* sailed on her sea trials to the Pool of London where she was greeted by the Canadian High Commissioner and she sailed under Tower Bridge.'

When John Cabot returned to Bristol on 5th August l497, he was acclaimed as a hero by his sponsors. King Henry VII rewarded him with the princely sum of £10 and a pension of £20 a year and suggested he make a return journey to find out more about the new continent. Although he did lead a larger expedition the following year, little is known of it, and John Cabot and the five ships that sailed were never seen again.

Records show that the *Matthew* joined the normal merchant ships transporting goods to and from England, Ireland, France and Spain, and continued to serve the port of Bristol for probably fifteen years after her famous voyage.

The replica of the *Matthew* was the centrepiece of Bristol's International Festival of the Sea. Building has taken just over two years, using methods from the time when the original *Matthew* was constructed.

Although no contemporary drawings of the original *Matthew* exist, the renowned naval architect Colin Mudie undertook extensive research into ships of the period and designed what everyone involved with the *Matthew* project believes to be an as authentic as possible three masted square-rigged caravel.

Colin Mudie onboard the *Matthew* during her first voyage in Bristol City Docks.

# Designing the Matthew

Colin Mudie RDI, CEng, FRINA

John Cabot's Matthew was built at what might be considered as one of the top periods of wooden shipbuilding. Skilled craftsmen constructed seagoing vessels able to make their way across oceans and withstand great storms, largely without the benefit of the metal fastenings on which we rely so heavily these days. Timber was the only material available to them for building ships and it was picked and felled and treated with the greatest of care. The various bits of ship were notched and hooked in such a manner that it needed only wood pegs (or treenails) to hold everything together, ready to carry crew and cargo from port to port for many years. What is more the ship was planned for economic production using parallel planks all of the same widths. This was not only economic for the builders but meant that she could easily be repaired from the minumum of onboard spares.

The builders of the new *Matthew* put her together in what we believe to be the manner of the original builders and we were very pleased indeed when she arrived in Newfoundland looking as if she was brand new, without a single crack in the seams or having made a drop of water.

Designing the new *Matthew* was in many ways a revelation. In particular we found that the technical level of such vessels was very high indeed – in some respects well in advance of our modern vessels. Nowadays, we tend to make our vessels longer in order to raise their maximum speeds. In the time of Cabot the pressure on the designers (who were also the builders) lay with the dangers of light winds. A failing breeze, when the ship may be being carried by strong tides amongst banks or rocks was of at least as great concern as safety in the strongest winds when the ship's master had plenty of power. So the ships of the period were made short and deep and well rounded for the best slow speed hydrodynamics and given what we would now consider enormous sails. For our *Matthew* we had, in any case, to fit her with an auxiliary engine for safety when working through shipping lanes. With no practical need for the excesses of sail you can see that we reduced her areas closer to modern practices in the interests of the many and varied crew she would take to sea.

Many of the contemporary illustrations of square-rigged sailing ships show them with 'billowing' sails. It is interesting that this 'kiting' of the sails was deliberate in order to reduce the angle of the heel, and therefore increase the efficiency of the hull. It is also interesting that square rig was chosen for its windward efficiency, partly because the extra area produced hull speed, but also due to the way in which the yards (holding the square sails) could be swung nearly fore and aft against the rope rigging to the mast.

Square rig was the choice of explorers such as Cabot and developed by them, as they explored the world and its oceans. With the sails balanced across the mast the handling loads were small for the area which could be set. More important was the ability of a many-masted, square-rigged vessel to manoeuvre, to back, fill, stop, start and even reverse very quickly. The value of this when steering in towards a strange and unknown coast can be appreciated. The generation of the *Matthew* was therefore one that saw a very significant increase in seafaring ability.

On 20th May 1994, HRH The Prince Philip, Duke of Edinburgh, Patron to The Matthew Project, officially laid the keel of the *Matthew*. After arriving at Redcliffe Quay in the Lord Mayor's horse-drawn carriage, he used St. John Hartnell's auctioneer's gavel to tap the keel, which was then blessed by the Bishop of Bristol. It was an auspicious start for a project and a vessel that would excite more and more attention as she neared completion.

The replica *Matthew's* designer, Colin Mudie, discusses with two of her builders how the planks will be set in place. Many will be put in a special 'steamer' first, the hot moist air will make the planks more flexible: then, starting from the bottom of the hull, near the keel, the building team will pull them into place and secure them.

## *In the summer of 1995 this is still a dream . . .*

*Matthew* with all sails set: from the top they are the Main Topsail, the Mainsail, the Foresail and the Spritsail. Hidden behind them all is the triangular lateen sail on the Mizzen mast. The Mainsail and Foresail are fitted with sections of sails called bonnets which can be removed for strong winds and make the sails smaller. The square sails are all lashed onto yards, wooden poles along the top of the sail. These can be pulled around by the braces (ropes from the end of the yard running down to deck) to turn the sails to best catch the wind.

From inside, the intricate structure that makes up the vessel can be seen; from the vertical frames to which the horizontal planks of the hull itself are secured, to the right angled hanging knees. These in turn support the deck beams on which the deck is resting.

Twenty six oak trees have been used for the timber of the *Matthew*. Decking has been made from Douglas pine, and other parts from larch. A 75-foot Douglas fir was used for the ship's mainmast.

In determining the shape of the *Matthew's* hull Colin Mudie was much helped by his involvement with the raising and research of the Tudor ship the *Mary Rose*, whose hull form he describes as the most sophisticated and beautiful, and 'streets ahead of what naval architects have been drawing for the last 100 years'.

September 1995: as thousands of people gather to watch, the *Matthew* is prepared for her launching. Since there is no slipway at Redcliffe Quay she will be lowered in by crane. Rising behind the canopy is the spire of St. Mary Redcliffe Church. After launching *Matthew* will be returned to stand on the quayside again and be completed.

Her topsides planked, and the rails under construction, the *Matthew* changes from a hull into the ship she will become. Below decks the accommodation is also being completed.

What would a skilled shipbuilder, working in a prosperous port such as Bristol and master of an extensive 15th century technology with money, skills and material available to him, put together for a sensible and skilled seaman explorer such as John Cabot?

The storage needed in the *Matthew* was worked out by a rule of thumb, comparing what modern man might need for such a journey and increasing it, taking into account the less convenient packaging and spoilage of the food of Cabot's time, and adding volume needed to store spare rigging and planking timber, anchor cables, crew sleeping and clothing space, and room for booty and trade goods.

Without sails, masts, spars, or even a bowsprit, from just six metres the bow of the *Matthew* is an impressive sight.

*Matthew* is equally striking from astern: the oak rudder four metres tall has four iron bands. The horizontal timbers on either side are the yoke. The braces from the top of the yard holding up the mainsail will come down to here, allowing the crew to move the sail to catch the wind.

Every aspect of authenticity in the *Matthew's* reconstruction would, of course, have been impossible, and present-day safety requirements deemed that features like the poor quality iron hull fastenings of the period were brought up to date by replacing them with aluminium bronze ones. Modern systems of propulsion, and safety-conscious fuels and equipment have also been used.

The *Matthew's* maiden voyage took her first to Falmouth, then on to Portland, Poole, Lymington, Chatham and London. She returned to Bristol via Portland, Plymouth, Falmouth and Penzance.

Looking back underneath the aft castle shows the full view that the helmsman would have had. Modern requirements for a chartroom, Captain's cabin and electronics will mean that the ship will have to be conned from the poop deck with the use of a whipstaff attached to the tiller. The rudder is controlled by a tiller (not fitted yet but the top of the rudderstock is just visible in the stern); unlike a modern tiller this one will be controlled with ropes and tackles rather than manually.

Watched by a large crowd of well-wishers, the *Matthew* is eased away for the first time from where she was built at Redcliffe Quay.

As if sensing the direction of the sea, the *Matthew* moves slowly through Bristol city docks, and in sight of Cabot Tower which can be seen on the skyline above her after castle.

*Opposite:* On the day she left Redcliffe Quay the replica *Matthew* passes Brunel's s.s. *Great Britain*, the first screw-propelled trans-Atlantic liner, which was launched in Bristol in 1843. In 1970 the s.s. *Great Britain* was refloated in the Falkland Islands and towed back to Bristol, where she has been restored, and is now on permanent display.

Following Bristol's International Festival of the Sea, the *Matthew* led the 'Atlantic Rendezvous' regatta to join Brest 96. The first leg of this voyage took the ships to Southern Ireland. During this trip the *Matthew* had her first taste of Atlantic gales and huge waves in the Irish Sea, and was forced to shelter in Cork before sailing on to Bantry Bay. The *Matthew* then headed for Penzance where she took part in the West Cornwall Maritime Festival before sailing for Charlestown, in Cornwall, and then on to Brest 96, the huge maritime festival in Brittany.

Since attending these festivals in the summer of 1996 the *Matthew* has called at Lymington, Cowes, Portsmouth and Hamble, where she underwent some minor modifications. During her trip back to Bristol she called at Plymouth before finally sailing, once again, up the River Avon to the City Docks, to be made ready for her epic voyage in 1997.

On board for the first trip are the men who had built her; their hard work, which had begun with the lofting and the keel laying, and continued until the *Matthew* took shape, grew and became a vessel, had finally finished.

A job well done. The *Matthew's* team of shipwrights, headed by Mike Blackwell (second from right) celebrate her first short voyage, down the River Avon, with a drop of liquid refreshment.

At the end of four fabulous days, the dedication of the *Matthew* and the finale of Bristol's International Festival of the Sea. The *Matthew*'s skipper has received his sailing orders and the replica of John Cabot's ship eases away from the dockside to acknowledge the cheers from tens of thousands of well-wishers, and to salute the city where she was built.

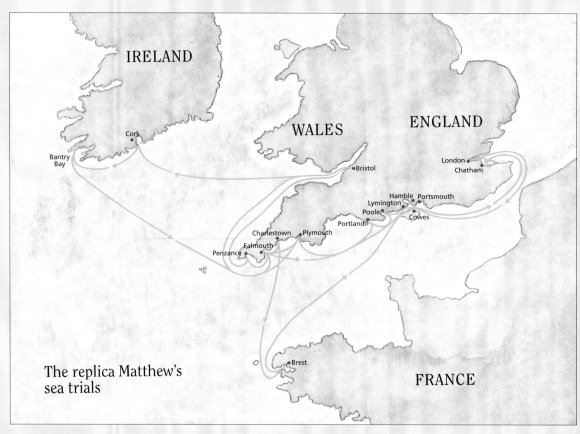

The replica Matthew's sea trials

IRELAND

WALES

ENGLAND

FRANCE

Cork

Bantry Bay

London
Chatham

Bristol

Hamble    Portsmouth
Lymington
Poole        Cowes
Portland

Charlestown    Plymouth
Falmouth
Penzance

Brest

We appoint you COMMANDER of our caravel

# Matthew

built by the skills efforts and industry of the City of Bristol in Partnership together with Commerce of this venerable Kingdom to the purpose of remembering & marking the life and times of our right celebrated ancestor John Cabot and his momentous Voyage to the New Founde Landes these 500 years passed.

You shall next Year follow his wake to the West and to those same New Founde Landes to join his descendants and all peoples in marking his adventure.

Now in this our MATTHEW's Maiden Voyage we desire you to repair on board her at Bristol Harbour with your ship's company not exceeding Twenty in number yourself included and embrace the first opportunity of sailing and make the best of your way to Castletown Bere in the Bantry Bay on the Coast of Ireland.

Thence to the Port of La Rochelle in the Republic of France and afterwards to the ancient Town of Penzance In This Kingdom. Afterwards to L'Aber Wrac'h and finally on the 12th of July to Brest in the Ancient country of Brittany where you shall with all state and dignity represent ourselves to the City of Brest and the Navy of France in their great and timely festivities of the sea which so inspired us.

You shall rest no more than the appointed time in each harbour and shall between proceed at all speed upon your way in this our ships maiden Voyage.

In all places manners and times you shall ensure that your crew & yourself do conduct yourselves in a sober and industrious and pleasing fashion. Furthermore you shall honestly and with due responsibility and care carry our Greeting to each place, instructing and informing the populace in Peace Goodwill and the History of our John Cabot.

You shall in this endeavour transport no cargoes or in other wise trade but shall Bring the Greeting of The City of Bristol and this Great Festival of the Sea to the peoples you shall meet and to their reporters and messengers. The Gifts we have provided and those of which this Great City have entrusted to your care shall be delivered undamaged into the hands of those to whom they are destined.

Upon your return to this our City you shall diligently prepare yourself and your crew to the task of your Newfoundland Voyage to commence on 2nd May 1997.

## We wish you God speed and farewell

## The International Festival of the Sea

In May 1996 the historic city docks in Bristol hosted eight hundred classic and traditional craft, from tall ships to steamers, and from yachts to trawlers, for an unforgettable four days – to celebrate five hundred years of exploration and endeavour at sea – and the completion of the replica *Matthew*.

All around this historic site, in the heart of the city, modern Bristol meets with its distinguished past.

The harbour itself, developed in the early nineteenth century, contains many important relics of the city's maritime past, where ships, built 'Shipshape and Bristol fashion' right up to the 1970s, became a byword for seaworthiness and efficiency.

The spire of St. Mary Redcliffe Church, described by Queen Elizabeth I as 'the noblest church in the land', soars above the eastern end of the docks. It is here, close to this famous landmark, that a team of westcountry shipwrights have built the replica *Matthew*.

The Cathedral on College Green and the tower of Bristol University share the horizon with the Cabot Tower on the northern side.

To the west of the docks the s.s. *Great Britain* is an impressive reminder of Bristol's shipbuilding past.

Nearby the Industrial Museum houses a remarkable collection of Bristol memorabilia, telling the story of maritime Bristol right up to the first flight of Concorde.

Bristol has a long history and is a city worth experiencing.

Read by St. John Hartnell to skipper David Alan-Williams on the night of 27th May at the International Festival of the Sea.

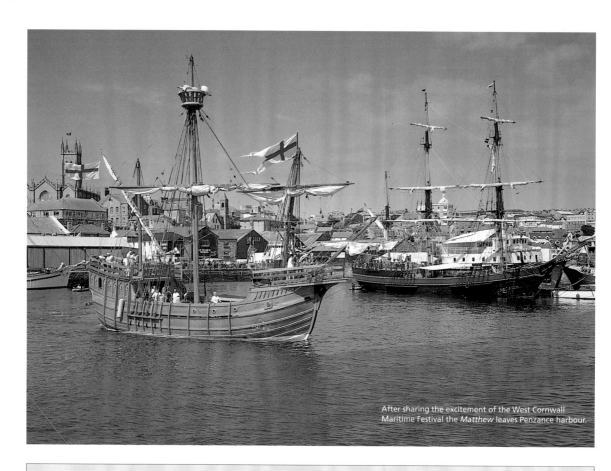

After sharing the excitement of the West Cornwall Maritime Festival the *Matthew* leaves Penzance harbour.

 ## ACCOMMODATION

### BELOW DECK

The accommodation space below the weather deck is divided into three compartments by two watertight bulkheads – the forward, main and aft compartments. These compartments are accessed by three companionways through hatches in the weather deck. There is also access between the main and aft compartments via a watertight door.

### Forward Compartment

Equipped with storage bins, shelving and workbench.

### Main Compartment

Main sleeping accommodation area equipped with eighteen pipe berths with canvas bases. There are two enclosed heads port and starboard at the aft end of the compartment, each equipped with a toilet and hand basin. The port heads compartment is equipped with a shower.

### Aft Compartment

Galley with propane gas cooker, sinks and worktop situated on the port side forward with separate food serving area and washing up area to starboard. Racking and refrigerator also to starboard.

The aft end of the compartment is fitted with seating and a dining table for the crew. There are two pilot berths outboard of the seating.

### ABOVE DECK

### Main Deck Forward

There is stowage for anchors, and mooring lines under the forcastle.

### Main Deck Aft

There are cabins port and starboard on the main deck beneath the poop deck. Starboard side is the navigator's cabin equipped with a chart table, main electrical panel and navigation instruments.

Port side is the Captain's cabin equipped with a sleeping berth and stowage lockers.

Aft of the cabins is the main steering position.

### Poop Deck

The upper steering position is on the poop deck, which is accessible via two companionway ladders from the main deck.

# The voyage begins . . .

On 2nd May 1997 the replica *Matthew* set off for Newfoundland. After a service in Bristol Cathedral attended by HRH The Duke of Edinburgh there was a procession to the *Matthew*, moored in the City docks, where the Bishop of Bristol blessed the crew and wished them *'bon voyage'*. To the sound of the bells of the Cathedral and St. Mary Redcliffe Church ringing out in celebration, and the cheers from huge crowds, the *Matthew*, with HRH The Duke of Edinburgh at the helm, moved slowly towards the Cumberland Basin on the first short leg of her voyage.

Departing the Cumberland Basin on the following day, and accompanied by a flotilla of other ships, the *Matthew* continued down river beneath the explosions of thousands of firecrackers which had been suspended from the Clifton Suspension Bridge, then on through the spectacular Avon Gorge. As the *Matthew* slowly left Bristol behind her Concorde flew low overhead – a final magnificent tribute from an aircraft that has meant so much to the people of Bristol.

Each day of the voyage the captain's log could be examined via the Internet so people around the world could track the *Matthew's* progress. The following are extracts from the log and give a fascinating glimpse of life onboard the *Matthew* during her historic seven week crossing of the Atlantic.

Two days after leaving Bristol the *Matthew* was off Milford Haven. *Matthew's* skipper, David Alan-Williams, had hoped to shelter in Milford Haven, after hearing that gales were forecast, but the wind direction changed so quickly that they had no choice but to ride out the storm at sea.

*'It is all we can do to hold position as the sun sets and we are beating about in strong winds of 35 to 40 knots, with driving rain squalls. There is no option but to stay outside and ride out the gale with some shelter under the cliffs.'*

At daybreak on 6th May David Alan-Williams decided that it was a lost cause to try to shelter in Milford Haven. With a forecast of winds easing to force 4 or 5 the *Matthew* headed towards Ireland.

**The Crew**

*Back row (left to right):*
**Russell Owen** aft deck hand & ship's chaplain,
**Kevin O'Leary** fore mast hand aloft,
**Steve Greenwood** main deck hand,
**Luke Porter** main deck hand,
**Terry Nash** port watch captain,
**David Alan-Williams** skipper,
**Russell Thiessen** starboard watch captain,
**James Roy** main mast hand aloft,
**Peter Zimonjic** fore mast hand aloft,
**Nigel Church** fore deck hand and
**John Jack Smith** aft deck hand.

*Front row (left to right):*
**Orlando Stuart** main deck hand,
**Nick Craig** main mast hand aloft,
**Paul Venton** fore deck hand,
**Gerry Gibbs** main deck hand,
**Mark Chislet** main deck hand,
**Matthew Wills** main deck hand and
**Chris LeGrow** main mast hand aloft.

*Inset:*
**Martin Pick**, fore deck hand, with his wife, on arrival in Bonavista.

Six of the outward going crew also sailed the return Atlantic crossing. These were David Alan-Williams, Terry Nash, James Roy, Mark Chislett, Nick Craig and Paul Venton.

Three days later the *Matthew* was 'beating about' the Celtic Sea, attempting to catch a favourable wind towards Cork harbour. She made Crosshaven in the evening of 10th May. By noon of that day the ship had logged 338 miles.

After two days of Irish hospitality the *Matthew* slipped away from Crosshaven and headed westward again.

By 14th May the *Matthew* was preparing to leave her last port of call, Castletown Bere.

*'Now is the time for final preparations, buy last stocks of fresh food and getting done those jobs that take five minutes on a level keel in harbour rather than an hour at sea.'*

The crew enjoyed their last supper ashore on the 16th May and at 1.30 pm they left Castletown Bere. By 6 pm the ship had passed Dursey Head and Bull Rock. There was now no more land in sight.

By noon on 17th May the *Matthew* had travelled 618.7 miles but with no wind she was becalmed. This gave the crew a chance to check the boat's systems.

Potential problems were envisioned when the starter motor, used to recharge the batteries, failed. The *Matthew* crew

The crew, dressed in costume of Cabot's time, have walked the short distance from Bristol Cathedral and now have just a few paces to go before boarding the *Matthew* in the City docks. Huge crowds have gathered to share the excitement, crowds which extended along much of the waterfront between the city and Cumberland Basin, and beyond.

As the *Matthew* comes out of Cumberland Basin lock, towed by rowing boats from HMS Victory, Cutty Sark and the Atlantic Challenge her swivel cannons roar into action in response to cheers from the banks of the River Avon. An estimated 200,000 people line the river.

# Television Coverage of the Matthew

Peter Firstbrook, Series Producer BBC Features, Bristol

The voyage of the Matthew was an important historic event and when plans were first proposed to cover the occasion for television, the unique nature of the voyage was of paramount importance. The historic significance of Cabot's exploration of North America was covered in the TV series with a variety of short drama sequences, filmed both on board the ship and on land, which told the story of maritime England in the 1490s. These were liberally sprinkled throughout the six programmes in the series and told the story of John Cabot's remarkable voyage.

But sailing a medieval replica ship across the stormy North Atlantic in 1997 is an extraordinary story in its own right, and from the very beginning I was keen to capture the experience of life on board the ship, as it happened – if possible, with live coverage for BBC1.

Working through the various options took several months. A live satellite link was the obvious solution, but this had several limitations. Firstly, we needed a satellite dish on the Matthew nearly 1.5 metres in diameter – something hardly appropriate for a traditional-looking medieval caravel. Secondly, the picture quality would have been poor. Finally, the satellite 'footprints' did not cover the central North Atlantic and we did not think we could maintain coverage.

The second option was more promising, but logistically very complex. It required the use of well tried and tested microwave links. These are used every day of the year when live interviews are inserted into news bulletins. The equipment is relatively cheap to hire and is robust to use in the difficult conditions experienced on board a sailing ship. The problem was the microwave link could only work over a maximum distance of five or six miles – a big problem as the ship was going to be as much as 1,000 miles from land!

The solution was aircraft. If a 'plane could find the ship in mid-Atlantic and then fly in a tight circular pattern around the ship for up to 90 minutes, we could beam pictures from the ship up to receiving equipment on the aircraft, which would return with the video material to the UK. The cost of hiring suitable aircraft for this task was far beyond my programme budget. But after months of discussions and negotiations, both the RAF and the Canadian Coastguard offered us this facility, free of charge as part of their training exercises.

The professionalism and good humour of both organisations could not be faulted. Every five or six days for over a month, RAF Nimrods flying from Kinloss in Scotland and later reconnaissance aircraft from the Canadian Coastguard in St. John's (Newfoundland), located the ship and established a microwave link, then recorded hours of video pictures beamed up from the Matthew. This was quickly returned to the BBC in Bristol, where the video material was edited and transmitted within a few days. The pictures were also seen in Canada and the USA.

Of course, none of this would have been possible without the good-humoured support of the skipper and crew of the Matthew, and the hard work of the BBC director and the cameraman on board the ship. Steve Greenwood and Orlando Stuart not only filmed life on board, day and night through calm and storm alike, but they were also full members of the crew with their own shipboard duties to perform. On board, they had a choice of five cameras and a state-of-the-art portable laptop editor. This tiny editing machine allowed them to pre-select the best material to be beamed up to the overflying aircraft; the machine itself was the very first prototype in the UK.

No doubt John Cabot would have been completely bewildered by the complexities of what we were up to in May and June 1997. But overall, I think we probably had it easy compared to what he had to face the first time around, 500 years ago.

The receiving equipment on board the RAF Nimrod aircraft, showing incoming pictures on the monitor.

Leaving the Clifton Suspension Bridge in the distance, the *Matthew* fires her cannons as she moves down the River Avon towards Avonmouth. The usually busy road along the Avon Gorge is closed to traffic, and instead filled with fairground rides and sideshows.

notified the shore support team and a replacement part was located in Ireland. It was transported by boat to the *Matthew* when she was about twenty five miles off Dingle Bay.

With repairs completed the *Matthew* began heading in a north westerly direction but gentle breezes meant that progress was slow. On 18th May the ship logged just 6·7 miles and by the end of the second week the total was 624.

The *Matthew* left the continental shelf on 21st May. She was now really on her way and bound for Newfoundland. 23rd May was a 'red letter day' for the ship and her crew, the day she recorded the best 24-hour run (123·9 miles) and passed the 1,000 miles mark.

28th May *'Today we are battened down and hove to in the toughest conditions yet. Feeling small and isolated in a big sea as the ship heaves, rolls and pitches.*

## Comments from some of the crew after their historic voyage

I'm only 21 and have crossed the Atlantic, visited hundreds of towns and met thousands of people, I've literally had the time of my life.

The experiences I have had are amazing and the memories awesome. The work's hard though and the chores could be boring and difficult in rough seas, but it was all worth it and given half a chance I'd do it all again.

**JAMES ROY** Main mast hand aloft

The Matthew – my pointed-ended garden shed!

**TERRY NASH** Port watch captain

The sheer adventure, the challenge, the danger - some of the same emotions that Cabot's crew must have experienced. The voyage presented me with an incredible opportunity, at the end of the twentieth century, to experience the fifteenth century - that never happened in a history lesson at school.

I loved the modern experiences too, particularly sailing down the St. Lawrence, awesomely sandwiched between gigantic tankers on one of the busiest seaways in the world! And then, of course, those universal experiences such as the fear, beauty and majesty of the icebergs - especially in the year of the Titanic movie.

**RUSSELL THIESSEN** Starboard watch captain

With waves breaking over the main deck there is relief, and praise for the way the architect Colin Mudie's design is riding the sea. She is a stout ship and John Cabot would, I am sure, be pleased to command her, just as I am.'

On the following day, the day that the *Matthew* passed the mid-way point between Ireland and Newfoundland, the storm had passed, but there was more rough water ahead!

31st May brought another gale. The winds, gusting at times to 60 knots, slammed the waves into the sides of the ship.

'Cascades of water flowed across the deck, looking for any small holes to get inside and land on the bunks. But amidst all the noise of the wind howling through the rigging and water rushing about, the Matthew *stood her ground and rode the waves with a calmness that reassured us all.'*

By the next morning the winds and sea had calmed but the storm had meant a setback for the *Matthew*. They were now further away from Bonavista than they were the day before.

The *Matthew* heads away from the Irish coast at the start of her voyage.

At the end of May the total miles logged was 1,617·9, and on 1st June the *Matthew* was about 800 miles off Bonavista.

*'Life on board a sailing ship at sea soon settles down to focus around the three main occupations; standing watch on deck, sleeping and eating,'* Captain's log, 4th June.

The *Matthew's* crew had company on 6th June. First contact was made with Canada, in the form of an Orion patrol aircraft of the Canadian Air Force. On 7th June the *Matthew* was 2,097·4 miles from Bristol, and seven days later the ship was approaching Canada's 200-mile limit. *'The countdown for arrival has started.'*

*'The grey, damp mist rolls back and forth, sometimes there is 200 metres visibility, occasionally as much as a couple of miles.'* Captain's log, 15th June.

On 17th June the Matthew drew closer to her destination with the help of a moderate breeze, and on 18th June, six days from landfall, the wind increased to 25 knots.

*'At 4 knots with the wind angle 70 degrees off the bow, it is some of the best sailing of the voyage.'*

The distance to go – 120 miles, but the last part of the voyage was proving difficult as the wind fluctuated.

*'The main yard and sail were lowered this morning as it gusted up to 30 knots. Now with it under 20, back on goes the bonnet, laced to the fore course and up goes the main yard to set the main course. There is more seaway than wind, slowing the ship and making it difficult to maintain steerage way. It is wriggle, wriggle, wriggle to keep the ship sailing, or else it may be necessary to re-write history for the arrival day.'*

Date: 24th June 1997 (final day's entry in my personal log)
Midday Position : 8 miles north east of Bonavista.
Wind Force: Gale 8
Direction: NNE
Weather: Driving rain, mist
Temp: -4°C

Of all the days of this voyage for the wind to blow a gale it does it today, our arrival day in the New Found Lands. We are motoring into Bonavista Bay with one stay sail up. It's very choppy, but we were still visited by a small coastguard boat to bring us some supplies. The supplies turn out to be deck cleaning materials – great! Of all things, it could have been some fresh food at least!

As it's rough and blowing a hooli on deck yours truly is again on galley duty – surprise, surprise! I always seem to draw the short straw.

Luckily the wind is nor'easterly which will push us straight into Bonavista harbour, of all the days for us to get a favourable wind!

All being well we will be on schedule for our meeting with the Heads of State and Her Majesty the Queen, along with 3,200 invited guests and dignitaries at 3 pm.

This afternoon is going to be like a zoo and I think it's last log entry time. What a voyage – I don't think I'll be wanting to do it again though, *Matthew* is a fine ship, and well built, but she does have a tendency to roll like a bitch!

**MARTIN PICK** Fore deck hand

What a glorious 'Au revoir' from the parish and Bristol. Fantastic send-off...and Irish hospitality; but now we are actually sailing the Atlantic.

Seasickness ? Yes, It worries me: am fearful too of being plucked overboard by the sea; as for galley duty? Maybe an angel will cross my name off the rota. But the awful moment of truth arrives: 2.30 am ship rolling crazily and avoiding the ugly feet of my mate above, I stagger out of my hammock. Russ! Galley duty! O, Sweet Jesus, no!

But, thanks to the brandy barrel, and an angel who gently said, 'Bread? looks like rice pudding', the day of doom ended. Did I tell you, shipmates as I opened the oven door Matthew gave an almighty roll, and the gunge slithered and squelched onto the deck - later you ate it, heartily, as bread!

Scrub decks, hoist main course, clean bilges, lower fore course, bonnet off, hands to wear ship: the bewildering array of sheets, clews, lifts, braces, martinets, chunky chicken, scrub decks: yes there were times when I was 'brassed-off','knackered' but whether on the graveyard watch, or the sheer bliss of diving into your hammock, the infectious humour of my shipmates will be my abiding memory.

The storm of 31st May was awesome. Billows frothing, huge walls of water, climbing, climbing: the wind shrieking like a thousand banshees, drunk, delirious, by the glorious might of nature's power; but when we were pooped – I knew fear; yet the sturdy little ship rode it all.

The warm, warm welcome of Newfoundland and Labrador. Thank you Skipper and shipmates for putting up with me.

Perhaps on my grave – 'He sailed on the Matthew'. But not just yet.

**RUSSELL OWEN** Aft deck hand & Ship's chaplain

The momentous discovery for Britain of Newfoundland in the New World bears significant importance to me. I went to sea at the very young age of fifteen on fore-and-aft fishing schooners, fishing the Grand Banks of Newfoundland for cod. Due to my experience of fishing the months of March and April when the gales were frequent, and the numerous voyages made across the Atlantic Ocean during the winter months via steam ship, sailing aboard the *Matthew* in 1996, and then crossing the north Atlantic in May 1997 were not exceptional trips. The only exception being, of course that she was a replica of a 15th century ship in which none of the crew had any seasoning sailing. It was definitely a learning experience for all of us! I personally would not have missed it for anything – a chance of a life time!

I thoroughly enjoyed the pleasure of meeting Prince Philip and being ship mate with him for a couple of hours while sailing down the River Avon. Meeting the Prince again in Newfoundland, accompanied by the Queen, was certainly the highlight of the voyage for me. How else would Jack Smith ever have had the opportunity to meet such high profile people had it not been for the *Matthew* project – I will always cherish those moments!

My warmest memories are those of the many wonderful people I met along the way, including the crew of eighteen strangers I sailed with for fifty-two days. Of course, by the end of the voyage our varied characteristics and personalities bonded us in a very close relationship. Our Captain, David Alan-Williams is a brilliant, experienced skipper who knows how to get every ounce of speed out of a sailing ship. I am pleased to have had the good fortune to sail under his command.

A trip of a lifetime, I wouldn't have missed it for the world!

**JOHN JACK SMITH** Aft deck hand

22nd June 1997. Russell Owen on deck as the *Matthew* approaches Newfoundland escorted by a Canadian coastguard vessel.

# The Matthew's visit to Newfoundland

David Redfern
*Media Director for the project and deckhand on the Canadian and American journeys*

'The *Matthew* arrived in Bonavista on a wet, cold, snowy, sleety, freezing day in June to be met by the Queen, Prince Philip, the Premier of Newfoundland, dozens of television crews, every VIP in Canada – and over four hundred Mounties to look after security.

The longest ever live broadcast in the history of Canadian broadcasting showed the arrival coast to coast. Peter Snow from the BBC and crews from HTV television in Bristol showed the arrival live in England, and international television networks broadcast one of the greatest spectacles in Canadian history. The *Matthew* had sailed 2,881·9 miles from Bristol to Bonavista in seven weeks and skipper David Alan-Williams had arrived exactly on time at three o'clock in the afternoon of Tuesday 24th June 1997, five hundred years after John Cabot had made the journey. It was the little *Matthew* and her crew that had first taken the English language to the north American continent. They had also achieved what Columbus never did, by sailing on to Nova Scotia, discovering the mainland of the continent.

The day after the *Matthew* arrived – a gloriously sunny day – despite being very tired from the journey but more so from celebrations that went on all night in the little town of 3,000 people, the ship and crew set sail again on a tour around the island that none were quite prepared for. We had a schedule and a calendar but none of the written information could have prepared us for the depth of feeling for the ship, the emotional arrivals and departures and the numbers of people who were to visit the ship. Newfoundland as an island looks small on the globe. It is in fact the size of England and Wales. To give a comparision, the north of the island is level with Bristol and the south is level with Bordeaux. The total population of the province of Newfoundland is 500,000 and more than half the population came aboard the ship.

24th June 1997. Unknown to the crew of the *Matthew* many members of their families flew to Newfoundland for a surprise reunion at the end of their trans-Atlantic voyage. Here a group of them, some in fifteenth-century costume, brave the rain and cold winds blowing across the quayside at Bonavista to hold aloft their welcome banner.

The arrival of the *Matthew* on 24th June 1997, five hundred years to the day after Cabot, marks the beginning of Newfoundland's Cabot 500 celebrations. During her forty-six day visit she will call at seventeen ports as she circumnavigates Newfoundland.

O, Buona Vista! For John Cabot, the arrival in Newfoundland in 1497 was a happy but unheralded moment. But in 1997 the replica of his ship is greeted by Her Majesty Queen Elizabeth II, HRH The Duke of Edinburgh, The Prime Minister of Canada, The Premier of Newfoundland and Labrador, thousands of guests – and tremendous excitement. She met in Bonavista by a flotilla of boats, many of which have sailed from Toronto.

For the master of the ship and the remaining crew – Terry Nash, Russell Thiessen, James Roy and Jack Smith – with Laurel Alan-Williams and myself now joining the ship for the forty-six days voyage to seventeen ports in Newfoundland and Labrador, it was an adventure that in parts, according to David Alan-Williams, made the Atlantic crossing seem calm in retrospect.

The Government of Newfoundland and Labrador had put an enormous amount of effort and money into the arrival and tour. We in Bristol had of course given the ship a tremendous send-off in May, and the other side were determined not to be outshone! Every facility that was needed was available. We had an escort for the journey by a Canadian Coastguard cutter,

*Top:* Just a few yards to go, and the first ropes are thrown ashore.

*Above:* HRH Queen Elizabeth, accompanied by the Premier of Newfoundland and Labrador, Brian Tobin, is introduced to the *Matthew's* crew after their arrival at Bonavista.

Peering at the planks of wood between me in my bunk and the fifty foot waves on the other side as they exploded like a cannon against the side of the Matthew, making the whole ship shudder, reminded me to appreciate the power of the ocean and our vulnerability as we steadily attempted to pass over it.

Sailing on the Matthew to Newfoundland was a bit like going on a fairground ride for seven weeks!

I thank the skipper David Alan-Williams for awarding me a place amongst a great crew.

**PAUL VENTON** Fore deck hand

A unique way to meet and get to know eighteen other men, who will be friends for life. The highlight of the trip for me was the big storm - one hell of a way to meet the mighty forces of the Atlantic - on a medieval ship. Definitely a once in a lifetime experience (I hope).

**KEVIN O'LEARY** Fore mast hand

the *Grosswater Bay*, a Royal Canadian Mounted Police high-speed catamaran, the *Simonds* and a road crew onshore of over a hundred people. It was like touring as a rock band and royalty combined. At each port, the road crew had gone ahead and set up a giant mobile stage with deafening sound systems, podiums for the speakers, exhibition marquees, sponsors' hospitality pavilions and dozens of concession stalls for local traders.

Sometimes the logistics were horrendous. The *Matthew* would sail for thirty hours or so, but the road crew would have had twelve to fourteen hours on the road to get to the next port and set up, with only two or three hours sleep in between. The programme was so intense that we had to take care not to fall asleep during the official ceremonies. If one were on the 3 am watch, finishing at 6 am which was deck-scrubbing time, getting changed into medieval costume, loading and firing the cannons, then having an official

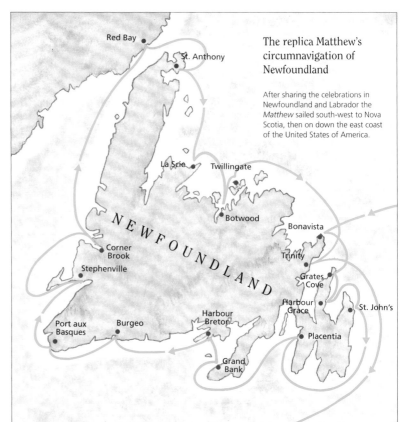

### The replica Matthew's circumnavigation of Newfoundland

After sharing the celebrations in Newfoundland and Labrador the *Matthew* sailed south-west to Nova Scotia, then on down the east coast of the United States of America.

The celebrations are over and the VIPs have left. Now Newfoundlanders and visitors from mainland Canada and the USA queue to visit the Matthew.

breakfast ashore, there would be no sleep at all until the next day.

Arriving in a port would see first of all small dories coming out to us, often at five in the morning. These tiny boats, with ninety horsepower engines, seemed to have the entire village in them, including dogs! As we got close to each port, every boat that could float came to greet us. This could amount to sixty boats, sometimes a hundred. The most was a hundred and forty-five – every one packed with people who were waving and cheering. It never failed to bring a lump to the throat to see the sheer love and affection expressed for the *Matthew* by an island people, who for seven years previously have had nothing but depression, misery and no jobs due to the cod fishing moratorium that has practically destroyed the province's economy. We would visit villages or islands where no one was employed, where the only industry, fishing and the processing factories were dead. We began to understand the powerful feeling after the first week, and to understand how important the *Matthew's* visit was, as a morale booster to the great people of Newfoundland.

For the crew of the *Matthew*, it was demanding. Because we were only six permanent crew, we relied on volunteer crews from each of the ports to make up the numbers. They had all applied to the government for a place in history, and they were naturally very excited and asked many questions. This often tested the crew's diplomacy and patience, having had only two or three hours sleep on each of the two days before arriving, as well as training the new crew on each leg of the journey, and doing very physical work. However, we could not fail to be overwhelmed by the generosity and hospitality that greeted us everywhere we went and took our part in the adventure with renewed enthusiasm, fired by the excitement of the new crews that joined us.

Going ashore, David Alan-Williams and the entire crew would be cheered, with lines of people touching us and shaking hands. Children, with eyes wide open at the sight of a bedraggled crew in medieval costume might think we were pirates as we staggered ashore. Usually

Salute from the skies. The Royal Canadian Airforce Snowbirds aerobatic team display in the clear skies above the *Matthew* as she lies in Bonavista harbour.

*Above:* The *Matthew* at Harbour Grace, the third port of call on her circumnavigation of Newfoundland.

*Right:* With a new Canadian crew on board, the *Matthew* sails through Conception Bay on her way from Harbour Grace to St. John's.

the first item on the agenda was a performance by the Rising Tide Theatre that was a 'Landfall Re-enactment' ceremony. The words and songs became engraved in our minds. Next would be a welcome from the local mayor and reception committee. There were church services to attend and in the French communities, these were conducted in two languages.

On each leg of the journey, as well as volunteer crew, we had on board at least one Member of the Newfoundland House of Assemblies, and perhaps a Minister and Members of the Canadian Federal Parliament who would give their impressions of the journey. Local musicians usually had written a song or two especially for the occasion. We would then have a preview of the evening concert performed by a tremendous group of boys called the 'Irish Descendants'.

After the ceremonies, with usually eleven speeches, (the record was eighteen) the crew would look for a shower and change of clothes. They would then return to the ship to welcome the visitors. The ship was open to the public from 10.00 am to 10.00 pm. During this time, various

Imagine a giant cork in the Atlantic, and living on that cork for six weeks. Then you might get some idea of the motion. On a bad day, life on board was like prison with a chance of drowning, only with less sleep and worse food.

During a force ten gale half way across the Atlantic the sea was the most humbling and beautiful thing I have ever seen.

Take one replica caravel. Roll constantly from side to side and apply generous amounts of cold sea water and spray. Add nineteen strangers and isolate from civilisation for six weeks. Ensure a slippery deck, hundreds of whistling ropes, some big waves and bad weather. Reduce crew from sleep. Not the recipe for a piece of cake, but a good way to learn about filming on boats.

In fact, initial impressions of jail with a chance of drowning have improved with time. Getting enough sleep is still a problem however as the motion makes co-ordinated movements more tiring than usual. Digital video is a good format to choose, with one hour tapes and compact equipment. A wide angle lens is essential – a tripod is not. A dedicated storm camera is a good idea as are waterproof cases, ratchet straps and clothing you can move in. Keep accessories to a minimum. With wind speeds in excess of 60 mph, think about sound recording too.

**ORLANDO STUART** Main deck hand

During the voyage Orlando sent a message in a bottle from the *Matthew* near Newfoundland. It was discovered four months later on Tiree, the most westerly island of the Outer Hebrides, having travelled over three thousand miles.

The *Matthew* arrives in St. John's to a spectacular welcome at the end of the first part of her epic voyage.

St. John's for Canada Day. The *Matthew* shares the harbourside with NATO warships, who are also visiting for the celebrations.

around the decks of the *Matthew*. There were times when the crew felt exhausted to a state of collapse, but of course, we smiled and kept the show on the road.

Newfoundland is a vast country with huge distances without change of scenery or sign of people or animals. We sailed past spectacular 1,000ft high cliffs with waterfalls cascading down into the sea. Hump-back whales came to look at us and at times they were so close we could see that they were looking at us very carefully with their large soft eyes as big as grapefruits. Whales became so much of a normal occurrence that David Alan-Williams would only be drawn to have a look if we could see them dancing! There are only two places in the world where you can see whales at such close quarters with giant turquoise blue icebergs for a backdrop. The other country is Chile, and I would totally recommend anyone who wants an offbeat vacation to go to Newfoundland. The flight time is only an hour longer than from London to Athens, and although Newfoundland is in North America, it is only halfway to New York.

At the port of Botwood, we saw the first transatlantic airport – or more correctly seaplane port. Here was a delightful wooden shed that was the original departure lounge. It housed a museum with photographs of the great Hollywood stars and politicians such as Churchill and Sir Anthony Eden, going out to the giant Imperial Airways Clipper flying boats for the journey to Britain, or on to the United States. A Catalina coastal

crew members had separate engagements ashore. It might be a lunch and talk at the Rotary Club, a meal with the Lions or a tree-planting ceremony for the skipper, and then dinner and more speeches at night, frequently with a play, concert and more speeches until the early hours. Aboard ship, 3,000 visitors a day walked

patrol aircraft, familiar to every schoolboy in England just after the Second World War is parked on the slipway that was built for the great seaplanes of yesterday. It made me wonder if things had really improved after seeing photographs here of passengers onboard these old aircraft sitting at tables, being served with silver cutlery on porcelain plates, and in great style before retiring to a private bedroom on board the aeroplane!

Each town that the *Matthew* visited had its own special character and a reflection of its origins. We would visit French ports, Basque towns, Irish areas and English West Country villages. Almost the first greeting on arrival in St. John's was a fisherman asking 'Where you to, boy, where you at?' just as if I was back home in the West Country. The skipper said at one speeching engagement 'I was listening to the marine radio last night, to fishermen chatting to each other. It could have been, by the accent, anywhere in Cornwall, and as usual, being fishermen, I didn't understand a word they were saying!' The West Country accent is as strong, if not stronger than that spoken at home now!

It was this link to the 'old country' that again was so important. People could look at the *Matthew* and see where they had come from. They could see how this community had developed from those early fishermen from Bristol, from Ireland, from the Basque regions and from France who had come to the island. For me, it was a strange experience to see in reverse, where we had gone, and to see so many living links to how our ancestors lived in those hard days of fishing and salting cod. After six weeks, like all great journeys, we soon began, sadly, to realise that we had only two or three ports left to call. As we left Red Bay in Labrador heading back to Newfoundland, crossing the freezing Labrador current in torrential rain with thick fog travelling at thirty knots, and into some heavy seas we thought 'Yes, we know it's not supposed to be like this – with wind, fog and rain at the same time', but there it was. Suddenly the sun broke through and the wind went down to about

*Top:* A scene typical of the *Matthew's* approach to many of Newfoundland's coastal communities. David Redfern acknowledges the welcoming cheers from the small boats which have put to sea to escort the *Matthew* to harbour.

*Right:* The *Matthew's* crows nest shows a striking resemblance to Toronto's CN Tower despite five hundred years separating the design of mast and tower.

26 knots, David Alan-Williams – a racing skipper by nature – felt the omens were good so we put up all available sail and broke the world speed record for medieval caravels by reaching a magic 9.3 knots!*

*This was later surpassed on the return Atlantic crossing when the *Matthew* clocked 10·2 knots – surfing down some large waves.

Luckily, this was being filmed from the shore by a Canadian Broadcasting crew for transmission in a programme on the History of Canada being broadcast in 2000. It was without doubt the best footage of the *Matthew* we had seen on television so far. With sails fully up and on a very close reach, we finally headed into Trinity, our last port of call. It was estimated that 30,000 people were there to greet us and the same number when we left. The next day, after speeches, presentations and personal goodbyes, with our cannons firing from the ship, with fireworks from the shore, we slipped out of Trinity for a quiet few unannounced days in the capital, St. John's to make the ship clean and ready for the winter and the journey to Nova Scotia and Toronto.

I did not make the journey up the St. Lawrence, having to be back in England to work on the International Festival of the Sea in Portsmouth, but I flew back again to Hamilton, Ontario, and sailed the final leg into Toronto. This was the most awful part of the whole journey from a comfort point of view. For the first time, I was sick on board. The high wind, stinging sleet in the face, and the shallow fresh water caused the *Matthew* to buck like an unbroken horse. Items below that had survived the Atlantic were smashed apart and the twenty seven mile journey took seventeen hours. We arrived ten hours late at one in the morning in a high wind, lashings of rain, no welcome committee and then had to make the boat fast, find our hotel and feel that this was for now the end of the journey. Winter was creeping in fast and we had to find a safe berth. There was none of the euphoria we felt in the warm small ports of Newfoundland and unforgettable towns such as Bristol, Rhode Island in America.

*Top:* Safely home again! Having negotiated the Cumberland Basin lock the *Matthew* makes her triumphant return through the floating harbour, just a short distance from Bristol City Docks, where her historic journey had begun.

*Left:* A job well done. The *Matthew's* skipper, David Alan-Williams, steps ashore in Bristol to cheers from many of the Bristolians who had wished him and his crew good luck at the start of their adventure.

The end of the journey for me had arrived and three weeks later, in sub-zero weather, I took myself with David and Laurel Alan-Williams to the airport and thanked David with all my heart for giving me the chance to take part in the greatest adventure of my life. That little ship touched the hearts of millions and is very special to many people on both sides of the Atlantic. To end, let us not forget the generosity of Cornishman Mike Slade for financing the building the ship and the modern day merchants of Bristol led by St John Hartnell who made the dream a reality.'

Cape Bonavista Lighthouse

The *Matthew* spent the winter on Lake Ontario, Canada before her voyage back to Bristol. Starting with a trip down the St. Lawrence Seaway, she called at ports along the way. On the way to St. John's, Newfoundland, she made her way first to Prince Edward Island where she took part in the 150th Anniversary celebrations of the island joining Canada.

The *Matthew* left St. John's on 25th July 1998 and sailed for Douarnenez, France, which she reached, cannons roaring, on 13th August. After sharing the excitement of the French festival she headed for Portsmouth, and the 2nd International Festival of the Sea, before returning to Bristol on 12th September. Celebrations to mark the *Matthew's* return home were an echo of the festivities which Bristolians had enjoyed at the 1st International Festival of the Sea in 1996, and at the start of the *Matthew's* historic voyage in 1997.

One of the many whales that swam close to the *Matthew* in the seas around Newfoundland.

# John Cabot's 'New Founde Landes'

'In 1497 Newfoundland was 'officially' discovered by John Cabot and in 1583 we were claimed for England by the adventurer Sir Humphrey Gilbert. It was the search for new lands which brought the mariners of Europe to our doorstep, but it was the riches of the sea which kept them coming' . . .

Newfoundland & Labrador Travel Guide

The spectacular icebergs that float past Labrador and Newfoundland every summer originate from Greenland's ice cap. It is thought that between 10,000 and 30,000 icebergs drift south each year, and that around 1,500 of these make it all the way to the warm waters of the Gulf Stream, where they eventually melt.

*Above:* The flags of Canada and Newfoundland and Labrador fly proudly from a yacht in Bonavista harbour.

*Left:* On the Avalon Peninsula, south of Placentia, is Cape St. Mary's which is home to one of the most spectacular seabird colonies in North America.

*Below:* Trinity, the last port of call for the *Matthew* and completion of her voyage around Newfoundland. She was greeted by 30,000 people when she arrived here on 8th August 1997.

*We are grateful to the following for their generous support, without which the production of this book would not have been possible.*

N. G. Bailey & Co. Ltd.

Brandwell Construction Ltd.

Bristol Evening Post & Press Ltd.

Bristol Water plc

Crest Homes Ltd.

Deloitte & Touche

Hartnell Taylor Cook

Hayes Parsons

Imperial Tobacco Ltd.

Lloyds Bank plc

McArthur Group Ltd.

Nat West Bank plc

Rolls Royce Military Aero Engines Ltd.

Capelcure Sharp

Trumps – Solicitors

*Credits for photographs:* David Redfern front cover (*top*), pages 19, 22 (*top*), 28 and 30 (*bottom*); Paul Venton front cover (*bottom*) and page 20; Colin Sanger pages 1 (*top*), 6, 11 (*top*), 13, 22 (*bottom*) and 29; St. John Hartnell page 2 (*top*); Steve Martin pages 2 (*bottom*), 10, 12, 14, 15 (*inset*), 16, 23, 25, 26 (*top*), 27 (*bottom*) and 31; Rosemary Mudie page 4; Max Mudie pages 5,7, 8 and 9; Bristol Evening Post page 11 (*bottom*); Martin Cheney page 15 (*top*); Peter Firstbrook page 17; Tony Marsh/Bristol Evening Post page 18; Orlando Stuart page 21 (*top*), Russell Owen page 21 (*bottom*); Roger Jonathan/Bristol Evening Post pages 24, 27 (*top*) and 32; Clyde Rose page 26 (*bottom*); Canadian Tourist Office page 30 (*top*). Maps: Steve Martin.